Original title:
Napping on Cloud Nine

Author: Benjamin Caldwell
ISBN HARDBACK: 978-9916-90-690-3
ISBN PAPERBACK: 978-9916-90-691-0

Calmness Cradled in the Sky

Soft whispers float on evening air,
A tranquil peace beyond compare.
Sunset paints the world in gold,
Stories of the day unfold.

Clouds drift slowly, gentle grace,
In this moment, time finds space.
Stars emerge, their light so clear,
Nature's song, forever near.

A silent breeze brushes my face,
Carried dreams, a warm embrace.
Eagles soar in twilight's glow,
On wings of peace, they seem to flow.

Calmness wraps the earth in night,
Guiding eyes to starlit sight.
In this stillness, hearts reside,
Cradled close, where love abides.

Echoing Lullabies of the Air

Whispers dance on twilight's breath,
Singing softly tales of rest.
Moonlight glimmers, shadows play,
Echoing lullabies at bay.

Each gentle breeze carries a tune,
Underneath the watchful moon.
Nature's chorus sings of peace,
As all worries find release.

Branches sway, a soft refrain,
In the dark, they sing again.
A melody of sweet escape,
Nurtured dreams in night's landscape.

Listen close, the air it sighs,
Wrapped in calm, the spirit flies.
Trust the whispers, let them guide,
In lullabies, forever hide.

The Sweetness of Weightlessness

In the calm of a silent sea,
Dreams drift softly, unanchored and free.
Stars whisper secrets, a tender embrace,
Time melts away in this tranquil space.

Floating high on a breeze's caress,
We find our refuge, we find our rest.
Hearts unburdened, in bliss we reside,
In weightless moments, let joy be our guide.

Shadows Gently Unraveled

As daylight wanes, a soft twilight gleams,
Shadows deepen, weaving our dreams.
Whispers of darkness, a comforting shroud,
In the dance of the night, we move unbowed.

Faint echoes linger, memories play,
Unraveling secrets the shadows display.
In the quiet corners, soft stories unfold,
Life in the twilight, a treasure untold.

Ambrosial Moments in the Air

A sweet fragrance drifts on the summer breeze,
Carrying laughter, dancing with ease.
Golden sunlight spills over fields wide,
In ambrosial moments, we take in stride.

Time halts gently, as joy fills the air,
With every heartbeat, we treasure and share.
Fleeting yet timeless, these days we adore,
In nature's embrace, we long for no more.

Tucked Beneath the Azure Veil

Under a sky of endless blue,
We find a solace so pure and true.
Clouds like whispers, soft as a sigh,
Tucked beneath this vast, open sky.

Dreams dance lightly, on horizons wide,
In this azure haven, we take our pride.
With hearts unburdened, we cherish the light,
Beneath the veil, everything feels right.

Drifting in Ethereal Silence

In twilight's soft embrace we float,
A whispering dream, a gentle note.
Stars captivate with shimmering grace,
As shadows dance in this sacred space.

The moon guards secrets, softly shines,
Wrapped in the stillness, where thought entwines.
In silent moments, our spirits soar,
Drifting through realms we can't ignore.

Each breath unveils a timeless sigh,
In the cosmic flow, where echoes lie.
Transcendent echoes beckon near,
In this ethereal silence, we disappear.

Moments of Bliss in the Stratosphere

Soaring high, away from care,
Among the clouds, we wander, rare.
Beneath the sun's warm golden kiss,
We find our peace, our moments bliss.

The world below, a distant hum,
In this expanse, our hearts succumb.
Floating free with weightless grace,
Embracing joy in this vast space.

Time drips slowly, like melting gold,
With laughter shared, our spirits unfold.
Together in this endless flight,
Moments of bliss ignite the night.

Cocooned in Nature's Embrace

Wrapped in leaves and gentle air,
Nature's cradle, beyond compare.
Birdsong dances, a sweet refrain,
In the forest's depth, we feel no pain.

Sunlight filters through the trees,
Caressing skin with softest breeze.
In petals' hues, our hearts align,
Cocooned in beauty, pure divine.

The stream's soft murmur, a lullaby,
As golden hours swiftly fly.
In nature's arms, we find our place,
A tranquil world, a warm embrace.

Weightless Whispers of the Heart

In quiet corners, love takes flight,
With every glance, a spark ignites.
Whispers dance upon the air,
Weightless dreams, a gentle pair.

Soft murmurs tease the sleeping night,
Fingertips brush, everything feels right.
In this tender realm where souls align,
Every heartbeat echoes, pure and fine.

Beneath the stars, our secrets share,
A symphony played, beyond compare.
Wrapped in warmth of feelings bright,
Weightless whispers guide us through the night.

Cushioned Comforts Above

In clouds of white, we find our peace,
Soft whispers call, our worries cease.
Gentle breezes stroke our skin,
Beneath the sky, we breathe within.

Each fluffy shape, a tale untold,
As sunlight spills in hues of gold.
With every sigh, our spirits soar,
Embracing dreams, we seek for more.

Suspended high, where thoughts take flight,
In soft embraces, we find delight.
The world below, a distant hum,
In tender arms, we're safe, we're calm.

Cushioned there, we drift away,
To hidden realms where hearts can play.
In every heartbeat, love is spun,
Above the clouds, we become as one.

Floating Thoughts on Cloud Bubbles

Thoughts like bubbles, float and gleam,
Drifting softly in a dream.
Carefree whispers on the breeze,
In the sky, they dance with ease.

Each bubble holds a wish so bright,
Reflecting colors, pure delight.
A gentle blow can set them free,
Carried far, like memories.

In this space where dreams collide,
Time is lost, and hopes reside.
Up above where worries fade,
Floating thoughts, a tranquil parade.

With every pop, new dreams appear,
A joyful laugh from skies so clear.
Cloud bubbles burst but never die,
They linger softly, drifting high.

Weightless Wishes in the Air

Wishes tossed like feathers light,
Carried onward, out of sight.
In the stillness, dreams take flight,
Fleeting moments, pure delight.

Graceful thoughts on currents glide,
In the open, hearts confide.
Weightless wonders, softly shared,
In the air, our hopes are spared.

Every sigh, a wish unfolds,
Stories whispered, never told.
Through the ether, sweet and fair,
Weightless wishes float and bare.

In this space devoid of fear,
The future shines, so bright and clear.
With every gust, our wishes soar,
In the air, we dream once more.

Sunset Snooze in the Heights

As day withdraws and shadows grow,
In twilight's arms, we ebb and flow.
The sunset paints the world in hue,
With tranquil strokes, the night bids adieu.

Above the hills, where silence reigns,
The fading light, a soft refrain.
With eyes closed tight, we find our rest,
In nature's cradle, we feel blessed.

Stars awaken, one by one,
In the blanket of night, we're all but undone.
Dreams intertwine with whispers low,
As time suspends, and darkness flows.

Peace envelops, a gentle tease,
In the heights, we drift with ease.
With every heartbeat, we embrace,
A sunset snooze, a sacred space.

Dreamy Retreat on Fluffy Shoulders

Beneath the clouds, we drift away,
In pastel hues, we find our play.
A sanctuary, soft and bright,
Where dreams take flight in gentle light.

With whispers sweet, the breezes sigh,
As sunbeams dance in azure sky.
In this embrace, the world feels small,
A haven where our hopes install.

We float on whispers, soft as night,
Each thought a star, each wish a kite.
In every corner, laughter blooms,
A cosmic joy that brightly looms.

So here we linger, hearts in tune,
As day surrenders to the moon.
On fluffy shoulders, dreams cascade,
In this retreat, our fears all fade.

Celestial Caresses

Stars twinkle in the velvet dome,
Each one a message, a place called home.
The night wraps softly, a tender embrace,
In cosmic whispers, we find our space.

Ethereal breezes brush our skin,
As we lose ourselves, letting love in.
Glimmers of hope, like fireflies roam,
In starlit gardens, we softly comb.

With every sigh, the universe glows,
In gentle touch, our essence flows.
Celestial bodies, a dance in the night,
Guiding our dreams with tranquil light.

So let the cosmos cradle us close,
In this vast night where our spirits chose.
Together we'll wander, forever to seek,
In celestial caresses, our souls will speak.

Comfort Wrapped in Airborne Slumber

Drift away on whispered sighs,
Where daylight fades and nighttime lies.
In cotton clouds, our worries cease,
Wrapped in warmth, we find our peace.

Through softest dreams, we intertwine,
With starlit paths, our hearts align.
In gentle waves of quiet night,
We float on hopes, our spirits bright.

The moon sings softly, a lullaby sweet,
As constellations weave tales at our feet.
With every breath, we draw in grace,
Comfort found in this sacred space.

So let us wander, souls set free,
In airborne slumber, you and me.
Together we'll rise, above the fray,
Wrapped in comfort, we'll find our way.

The Art of Daydreaming Aloud

In gentle moments, thoughts take flight,
We paint the day in colors bright.
With spoken wishes, dreams take form,
In sunny laughter, we weather the storm.

Our voices dance like leaves in breeze,
Creating worlds with effortless ease.
Each word a spark, each tale a thread,
In daydreams spun, our hearts are wed.

From whispered hopes to visions grand,
We sketch our dreams with a steady hand.
In joyous tones, our futures unfold,
The art of dreaming is precious gold.

So let us cherish this sacred sound,
In daydreaming aloud, together we're bound.
With each shared dream, our spirits rise,
In the canvas of life, boundless skies.

Dreaming Among the Fluffy Whispers

In fields where silence softly weaves,
Beneath the clouds that gently tease,
Awake yet lost in sweet delight,
I dance with shadows, out of sight.

Around me flutter secrets bright,
With every whisper of the night,
I close my eyes, the world I flee,
In dreams that drift like leaves from trees.

A treasure chest of memories dear,
Where laughter echoes, crystal clear,
Each moment captured, fleeting time,
In dreamy realms, I find my rhyme.

And in this place where wishes play,
I linger still, till break of day,
Among the fluffy whispers' grace,
I find my heart's most sacred space.

Slumbering in the Silver Skies

As twilight spills its silver hues,
I lay beneath the vast, dark blues,
The stars awake with gentle fight,
They whisper softly, good night, good night.

The moon, a guardian high above,
Cradles dreams with tender love,
In the stillness, I feel at peace,
While all my cares begin to cease.

Clouds drift like ships in the vast sea,
Carrying thoughts that swim so free,
I close my eyes and drift away,
In silver skies, I long to stay.

Tomorrow's light is far ahead,
For now, in beauty, I am led,
Slumbering deep till dawn arrives,
In dreams where waking heart survives.

Driftwood on a Pillowy Sea

Upon the waves of time I float,
A piece of driftwood, free of thought,
Where tides embrace with gentle sighs,
And whispers dance beneath the skies.

The sea, a canvas broad and wide,
Holds dreams and wishes in its tide,
Each crest a story, each trough a song,
In this vast world, I drift along.

The sunlight sparkles, diamonds fair,
While seagulls circle in the air,
I breathe in peace, a tranquil view,
A world so bright, an endless blue.

Among the waves, my troubles cease,
In harmony, I find my peace,
Driftwood floating, wild and free,
Upon the sea's vast melody.

Resting in the Aurora's Embrace

Beneath the glow of colors bright,
I find my soul in pure delight,
The aurora dances in the night,
A tapestry of warmth and light.

With hues of green and shades of pink,
I pause and breathe, I start to think,
In fleeting moments, stillness calls,
As nature's beauty gently enthralls.

Wrapped in this radiant display,
I forget the worries of the day,
Each shimmer whispers, drawing near,
In nature's arms, I have no fear.

The world beyond fades far away,
In auroral peace, I wish to stay,
Resting softly, lost in grace,
In the embrace of this wondrous space.

A Drift into Dreamy Skies

Soft whispers of the night,
Stars flicker, glowing bright.
Clouds cradle, gentle and wide,
As dreams begin to glide.

Moonlight spills a silver beam,
Carrying us through a dream.
Wrapped in hues of twilight's kiss,
We float in tranquil bliss.

Upward Bound in Slumber's Grace

Wings of night begin to fold,
In the cradle, warmth untold.
Rays of slumber softly tease,
Leaving whispers in the breeze.

Stars are secrets yet to share,
Quiet magic fills the air.
With each breath, we drift on high,
Upward bound in velvet sky.

Flights of Fancy in the Air

Feathers of hope begin to soar,
Chasing dreams we can't ignore.
Dancing through the night's embrace,
With laughter lighting up our pace.

In the shadows, wishes weave,
Knitted softly, we believe.
On the wings of silent night,
Flights of fancy take their flight.

Ethereal Embrace of Drowsiness

In the hush of evening's grace,
Time slows down in this safe space.
Tender thoughts like petals fall,
Ethereal whispers gently call.

Blankets of calm, a soft cocoon,
Cradled by the silver moon.
In drowsiness, we find our peace,
An embrace where dreams increase.

Driftwood of the Mind

Thoughts like waves, they gently sway,
Carried forth, they drift away.
Fragments lost, yet softly find,
Embers glowing in the mind.

Rafts of dreams on currents flow,
Whispers dance, they ebb and grow.
Scattered leaves on a silent sea,
Driftwood shapes my reverie.

Tides of memory pull me near,
Soft reflections, calm and clear.
In the stillness, echoes play,
Driftwood thoughts, they fade away.

Slumber’s Celestial Drift

Stars aglow in velvet night,
Cradle dreams in silver light.
Floating high on clouded streams,
Slumbered whispers weave the dreams.

Gentle lull, a cosmic tune,
Softly sings the dreaming moon.
In the hush, the heart takes flight,
Slumber’s drift in pure delight.

Galaxies spin in silent grace,
Time fades in this sacred space.
A tapestry of endless flight,
In slumber’s realm, we find our sight.

Daydreams in the Ether

Amidst the clouds, my thoughts will soar,
Floating high, forever more.
Colors blend in soft embrace,
Daydreams dance in endless space.

Fleeting visions, bright and bold,
Stories whispered, yet untold.
In the ether, minds ignite,
Daydreams bloom in morning light.

Wings of whimsy carry me,
Where the heart at last is free.
In the glow of thoughts divine,
Daydreams weave a bright design.

The Lullaby of Celestial Heights

In the stillness, stars align,
Singing songs of love divine.
A lullaby in twilight's grace,
Celestial heights, a warm embrace.

Echos shimmer, dreams take flight,
In the embrace of endless night.
Whispers tread on breezy air,
A lullaby beyond compare.

Galactic harmonies unfold,
Stories of the brave and bold.
In the cosmos, hear the sound,
A lullaby, eternally bound.

Daydreams in the Wisp of Twilight

In twilight's gentle, fading glow,
Thoughts linger softly, like a flow.
Shadows dance, as night peeks through,
Whispers of dreams, both old and new.

Stars awaken, blink and sigh,
While the world breathes a lullaby.
Lost in wonder, thoughts take flight,
In the wisp of gentle night.

Weightless Reveries of the Skybound

Clouds drift softly, high above,
Carrying dreams like a dove.
Wings unfurl in endless blue,
Weightless souls in skies anew.

Thoughts ascend with every breeze,
Dancing light through golden trees.
In this realm where time stands still,
Reveries float on sheer will.

Floating into the Soothe of Evening's Breath

Evening descends with a tender grace,
The world hushes, finding its place.
A sigh emitted from the trees,
As stars align and shadows tease.

Drifting deeper into the calm,
Nature wraps its soothing balm.
In this moment, peace we find,
Floating softly, intertwined.

Hibernating in Sunlit Softness

Beneath the sun's warm, golden light,
Resting softly, hearts take flight.
In a cocoon of gentle rays,
Lazily counting the sunny days.

Time flows slowly, sweet and soft,
In the embrace of warmth aloft.
Hibernating, dreams take shape,
In sunlit softness, worlds escape.

A Breath of Quietude Above

In the stillness of the night,
Stars linger, softly bright.
Moonlight dances on the trees,
Whispers carried by the breeze.

Clouds drift slowly, full of grace,
Time holds still, a warm embrace.
Thoughts like shadows gently roam,
In this quiet, I feel home.

Waves of calm wash over me,
Silent echoes, wild and free.
Here beneath the endless sky,
A breath of peace, a gentle sigh.

Gentle Haze of Afternoon Rest

Softly falls the afternoon,
Cloaked in light, a gentle tune.
Trees sway with a tender grace,
Time slows down in this sweet space.

Golden rays through branches play,
Casting shadows where we lay.
Silence wraps around the heart,
In this stillness, we’re set apart.

Open fields invite our dreams,
Where the world is not as it seems.
In the haze, we drift away,
Holding onto this bright day.

Midsummer Sky Tranquility

Clouds like cotton, soft and white,
Fluffy pillows in the light.
Beneath them stretches emerald grass,
In this calm, all worries pass.

Sunshine warms the happy land,
Nature whispers, pure and grand.
Lazy thoughts drift in the air,
Finding peace beyond all care.

Butterflies dance from bloom to bloom,
Filling the day with sweet perfume.
Time lingers, wrapped in delight,
In midsummer's gentle light.

The Weight of Whispered Thoughts

In the shadows, secrets sigh,
Echoes of the heart's soft cry.
Words unspoken hang like mist,
Longing for the touch we've missed.

Heavy hangs the evening air,
Thoughts like feathers, light as prayer.
Each one carries hopes and fears,
Softly drenching us in tears.

Yet in the quiet of the night,
The weight of words can feel so light.
Let them flutter, let them fly,
In this silence, we comply.

The Plushness of Skybound Whispers

Soft murmurs ride the breeze,
Cotton dreams beneath the trees.
Stars twinkle with gentle grace,
In the night's warm, tender embrace.

Feathers dance on quiet air,
Whispers linger, light as prayer.
Moonlight kisses twilight's cheek,
In the silence, secrets speak.

Clouds exchange their silent tales,
Drifting where the starlight pales.
Each breath held in soft delight,
In the arms of endless night.

Find the calm in softest sighs,
Where the whispering twilight lies.
In that space where dreams reside,
Feel the plushness, deep inside.

Floating on Bubbles of Joy

Bubbles rise with gleeful cheer,
Carried on by laughter's near.
Catching sunlight in their glint,
Moments pause, a perfect tint.

Each pop brings a heartfelt sound,
Joyful echoes all around.
Floating high, we drift and sway,
In this light, we're free to play.

Dancing on the painted air,
Every joy a treasure rare.
With each bubble, dreams are spun,
Floating high, we chase the sun.

In a world where mirth is shared,
Every heart must feel prepared.
To embrace the tender fun,
Floating 'neath the joyful sun.

Chasing Wisps of Tranquility

Soft and light, the wisps do roam,
Carrying us far from home.
In their embrace, all worries cease,
Finding solace, finding peace.

Windswept trails of gentle grace,
Whispers of a slower pace.
Chasing dreams on tranquil streams,
Wrapped in calm and silver beams.

Underneath the endless skies,
Clouds of stillness softly rise.
In their grasp, the world feels right,
Chasing peace in fading light.

Letting go of what we know,
In the stillness, let it flow.
Ride the waves of soft reprieve,
Chasing moments we believe.

Pillow Clouds in the Breeze

Pillow clouds drift ever slow,
In the sky, they weave and flow.
Soft as silk, they twirl and spin,
Cradling dreams as they begin.

Whispering winds that gently play,
Guide the clouds along their way.
In their shadows, laughter lies,
As we watch the dance arise.

Beneath the sky's expansive hue,
We find the world feels fresh and new.
Each cloud a promise, soft and white,
Guiding us through day and night.

Let us rest upon their fluff,
Finding joy in gentle stuff.
In the breeze, we feel so free,
Pillow clouds, just you and me.

Immersed in the Serenity of Soft Clouds

In gentle hues of pastel light,
Soft whispers dance, taking flight.
A lullaby drifts through the air,
Embracing hearts with tender care.

Beneath the vast, embracing sky,
The echoes of the day drift by.
With every sigh, the world feels right,
Wrapped in dreams that take their flight.

Floating high on cotton dreams,
Where the world is not as it seems.
In the cradle of a sunset's glow,
Serenity whispers soft and low.

Time slows down in this warm space,
With every breath, a slow embrace.
Immersed in peace, the spirit soars,
Finding solace forevermore.

Boundless Slumber Beneath Celestial Canopies.

Stars twinkle in a midnight dance,
Inviting all in a tranquil trance.
Where dreams weave softly through the night,
In slumber's hold, all feels so right.

Beneath the moon's soft silver glow,
A world awakens, calm and slow.
Each shadow holds a whispered wish,
In every heartbeat, a fleeting kiss.

The sky unfolds a velvet bed,
Where thoughts drift lightly, softly tread.
In boundless slumber, time is still,
Every moment, a heart to fill.

As dawn approaches, dreams will fade,
Yet in the quiet, memories stayed.
Under the sky’s vast, watchful grace,
A sacred journey we all embrace.

Whispers of Dozing Dreams

In the stillness, shadows play,
Cradling night, leading the way.
Whispers echo, softly stream,
As the world drifts into dream.

Moonbeams glide on velvet skies,
Painting stories with silent sighs.
Every moment, a treasure sweet,
In the tapestry of dreams, we meet.

Lulled by the song of a gentle breeze,
Floating softly among the trees.
A symphony of quiet grace,
In dozing dreams, we find our place.

Embracing night, the heart takes flight,
In whispered tones, we feel the light.
Awake in love, in dreams we bask,
Finding joy in what we ask.

Floating on Feathery Hues

Colors blend like a painter's brush,
Creating peace in a vibrant hush.
Feathered whispers kiss the ground,
In a world where dreams abound.

Through twilight's gaze, horizons gleam,
Wrapped in warmth, we dare to dream.
Each feathered cloud, a gentle sail,
Guiding us where heartbeats prevail.

Floating high on hopes that soar,
In a realm of nevermore.
Cocooned in softness, hearts unwind,
With every breath, the stars aligned.

In feathery hues, we drift away,
Lost in moments where shadows play.
Through whispers of the night, we find,
A sanctuary for the soul and mind.

Hush of the Dream Weaver

In the twilight's gentle glow,
Whispers float on breezy sighs,
Stars gently weave their tales,
As the world softly lies.

Velvet shadows play their game,
Lulling hearts to quiet rest,
A tapestry of dusk and flame,
Nestled in the evening's nest.

Dreams take flight on silken threads,
Carried by the moon's embrace,
Softly spoken, words unsaid,
In this sacred, tranquil space.

Rest now, dear soul, in peace,
Let the night your worries cease.

Lullabies for the Sky Wanderer

Above the clouds, the stars hum low,
A gentle tune to soothe the night,
Wanderers drift where wild winds blow,
Wrapped in dreams, their hearts take flight.

Each twinkling star, a wish in bloom,
Glowing softly in the vast expanse,
Casting away the shadowed gloom,
Encouraging the night to dance.

Moonbeams lace the haunted air,
Guiding souls in silver grace,
Lullabies whispered everywhere,
In the night's warm, sweet embrace.

So drift, dear dreamer, on this breeze,
Let the night bring peace with ease.

Clouds Cup the Heart

Billowing clouds, a soft embrace,
Cradling dreams within their hold,
Floating gently through open space,
Whispers of stories yet untold.

In the morning light they play,
Casting shadows on the ground,
A canvas where the heart will sway,
In this silence, peace is found.

As they weave the sky so high,
Each puff a promise, soft and true,
Cradling wishes meant to fly,
Painting skies in shades of blue.

With every breath, let worries part,
For these clouds gently cup the heart.

Fluffy Horizons of Tranquility

Across the horizon, clouds parade,
Soft and fluffy, bright and light,
They whisper secrets, unafraid,
In the warmth of the golden light.

Like cotton candy in the sky,
They drift and dance, a sweet delight,
Inviting hearts to pause and sigh,
Embracing peace in their soft flight.

Every hue a gentle brush,
Blushing pink and calming gray,
In this quiet, gentle hush,
We find the calm amidst the fray.

So let your spirit soar and play,
In fluffy horizons, peace will stay.

Day Escape on Gossamer Trails

In the light of dawn's sweet grace,
We wander through the dewy haze.
Paths of silk and secrets spun,
Chasing dreams beneath the sun.

Each step whispers tales untold,
Golden glimmers to behold.
Wings of freedom guide our way,
As we dance in the bright day.

Through the fields of emerald green,
Solitude's tender grace is seen.
Time drifts softly, like a breeze,
Carving joy among the trees.

With hearts aglow, we roam free,
In the warmth where we long to be.
Day escapes on gossamer trails,
In life's wonder, love prevails.

Lullabies of Cosmic Drift

Stars sing softly, night unfolds,
In the stillness, tales are told.
Galaxies spin in tranquil grace,
While time dances in space's embrace.

Dreams drift through the velvet sky,
Where wishes sparkle, never shy.
A universe of hope and light,
Guides the wanderer through the night.

Each heartbeat echoes in the void,
Whispers of love never destroyed.
Lullabies of cosmic drift,
Carrying souls with gentle lift.

In this moment, we find our peace,
Infinite stars that never cease.
Together we weave and sway,
In the cosmos, we find our way.

Fluttering into the Feathered Abyss

With wings unfurled, we take our flight,
Into the abyss where dreams ignite.
Feathers soft as whispered breeze,
Soaring high, lost in the trees.

Dancing shadows paint the air,
In the twilight, free from care.
Nature's marvels, wild and free,
Call to our hearts, where we long to be.

Each beat of wings a gentle hymn,
Filling the night, as lights grow dim.
With every flutter, we transcend,
Into the depths where colors blend.

The abyss sings, a siren's call,
To the daring, to the small.
Embrace the fall and let it be,
For in the depths, we find our spree.

Embracing the Breezy Calm

Gentle whispers through the trees,
A soft embrace from the summer breeze.
Clouds float slowly, drifting by,
Painting dreams across the sky.

In the stillness, hearts unwind,
A moment's grace, peace aligned.
Ripples dance upon the lake,
As tranquility begins to wake.

Sunlight filters through the shade,
Casting warmth where shadows played.
Embracing calm with open arms,
Surrendering to nature's charms.

In this haven, time stands still,
Focused on the heart's sweet thrill.
With every breath, the world slows down,
Embracing calm, our souls can drown.

Gentle Sojourn on Nimbus Shores

Upon the gentle waves we drift,
A soft embrace, a fleeting gift.
Clouds like whispers grace the air,
In tranquil hues of dreams laid bare.

The sun dips low, a golden glow,
Reflecting on the tides below.
Each breeze a tale, each wave a song,
Together here, we both belong.

Footprints left in moonlit sand,
In this serene, enchanted land.
Time slows down, the world seems bright,
With you, my love, beneath the night.

As starlit shadows softly play,
We find our peace, we softly sway.
With every breath, our spirits soar,
In this gentle sojourn, evermore.

Starlit Reveries with the Wind's Whisper

Beneath the sky, where stars align,
We share our dreams, your hand in mine.
The wind carries secrets from afar,
In whispers soft, under the stars.

Each twinkle sparks a hidden thought,
In cosmic tales, our souls are caught.
Lost in wonder, the night unfolds,
With every breath, a story told.

The moonlight dances, silver bright,
Kissing the earth, igniting the night.
With every sigh, the world stands still,
As starlit reveries weave our will.

In quiet moments, hearts entwined,
The universe reveals its mind.
As we embrace the night's sweet grace,
In every glance, a warm embrace.

Sleeping Among the Whispering Clouds

Drifting high on cotton dreams,
Among the clouds, the starlight beams.
With every whisper, the soft winds sigh,
As we drift gently, you and I.

The universe hums a lullaby,
Cradled in night, we softly lie.
Beneath the veil where shadows play,
In this serene, enchanted sway.

Time holds its breath as we explore,
The hidden realms of evermore.
Floating free, our spirits blend,
A journey without a single end.

With every heartbeat, the clouds embrace,
In their soft folds, we find our place.
Sleeping soundly, dreams take flight,
Among the whispers of the night.

Cushion of the Sky's Gentle Sway

Upon the crest of twilight's glow,
We lay on clouds, where breezes flow.
The sky, a cushion, soft and wide,
Embracing us with every tide.

Starlight flickers, a dazzling show,
As dreams awaken and softly grow.
The world below begins to fade,
In the warmth of the sky's cascade.

In this vast expanse, our laughter rings,
Like melodies carried upon soft wings.
With every thought, the cosmos plays,
A symphony in the sky's embrace.

Wrapped in twilight’s gentle fold,
We find adventure, brave and bold.
In this embrace where time can't stray,
We dance upon the sky's sweet sway.

Celestial Chronicles of Rest and Relaxation

Stars whisper tales of night,
Moonlight blankets our delight.
In the stillness, silence reigns,
Hearts find peace, release the chains.

Breezes carry dreams on high,
Clouds drift softly in the sky.
Time stands still, a gentle pause,
Nature sings without a cause.

Gentle tides of thought unwind,
Calmness wraps around the mind.
Every breath a soothing song,
In this rhythm, we belong.

Embrace the calm, let worries cease,
In this space, we find our peace.
Heavenly hues softly blend,
In the stillness, we ascend.

Tranquil Voyage on the Floating Horizon

Sail away on whispered dreams,
Where the sun and twilight beams.
Waves of calm dance in the light,
Guiding hearts through endless night.

Gentle breezes kiss the sea,
Every moment feels so free.
Horizon stretches wide and far,
A path aligned with every star.

Colors merge in evening's glow,
Softly guiding where to go.
Stars begin their nightly dance,
In this voyage, hearts find chance.

Anchor down in tranquil bliss,
In this peace, a gentle kiss.
Journey forth and let time flow,
Trust the path we do not know.

Dreamcrafting in the Heavenly Drift

Clouds are pillows, soft and light,
Crafting dreams that take their flight.
Colors swirl like morning mist,
In this space, the world is kissed.

Whispers echo in the breeze,
Carrying hopes like distant keys.
Every thought a starry thread,
Woven tales of dreams ahead.

Glimmers shine on pathways bright,
Guided by the moon's soft light.
Imagination takes its shape,
In this weave, we gladly escape.

Rise above the waking ground,
In the drift, our hearts are found.
With each breath, new worlds we paint,
In this dreamscape, we are faint.

Cozy Retreat in the Fluffiness Above

Nestled in the clouds so high,
Where the gentle breezes sigh.
Wrapped in warmth, we find our space,
In this haven, time leaves no trace.

Pillows soft as dreams can be,
Every breath a melody.
In this cozy, sweet embrace,
We surrender to the grace.

Sunlight trickles through the seams,
Painting canvas of our dreams.
Each moment feels like a hug,
In this retreat, love is snug.

Whispers float on air so rare,
Happiness is everywhere.
Floating high and free we roam,
In this fluff, we've found our home.

Cradled in Celestial Comfort

Stars twinkle softly in the night,
Wrapped in a blanket, pure and light.
The moon's gentle gaze, a soothing balm,
In this quiet space, everything feels calm.

Whispers of dreams drift on the air,
Carried by breezes, light as a prayer.
Each thought a feather, drifting free,
Cradled in comfort, just you and me.

The universe hums a lullaby sweet,
Painting our hearts with a rhythmic beat.
In celestial arms, we find our place,
Together we float through time and space.

Golden horizons stretch wide and far,
Guiding our paths, like a guiding star.
In the embrace of night’s tender glow,
Cradled forever in love's gentle flow.

Floating Dreams in the Blue

Above the clouds, where whispers weave,
Dreams take flight, we dare to believe.
Skyward we soar with hearts so light,
Floating on hopes, in the radiant light.

In the vast stretch of azure hue,
Every thought a vision, bright and new.
Waves of wonder rise like the tide,
In this boundless realm, we'll always glide.

Laughter dances on the playful breeze,
Crafting a world where we're at ease.
Among the stars, we twirl, we spin,
Floating dreams where the sky begins.

Painted in colors of dawn's embrace,
In this gentle light, we find our place.
With every heartbeat, our spirits align,
Floating forever, your hand in mine.

Enchanted by Skyward Whispers

Cascading thoughts drift on a sigh,
Whispers of wonder flutter and fly.
In the silence, secrets softly call,
Enchanted hearts rise, never to fall.

With every breeze, the stories unfold,
Tales of courage, of dreams bold.
Carried on currents, starlit and bright,
Skyward whispers dance through the night.

They beckon us forth to the great unknown,
In this realm, we are never alone.
With hope as our guide, we'll chase the sun,
Enchanted by whispers, our hearts become one.

In the fabric of night, our spirits entwine,
Magic envelops, a love divine.
Together we wander, through skies so wide,
Enchanted by whispers, forever our guide.

Soft Pillows of Imagination

Feathers of thoughts rest on soft pillows,
Imagination blooms, like a garden grows.
Each dream a petal, vibrant and bright,
Crafting a world where shadows take flight.

In realms of comfort, we play and explore,
Each inspiration, unlocking a door.
Ride on the waves of a fanciful stream,
Soft pillows cradle the essence of dream.

Whispers of magic swirl in the air,
Painting adventures, we share without care.
With laughter and joy, we sketch our fate,
Soft pillows of imagination await.

In the quiet corners of restful nights,
Dreams take shape in the softest lights.
Together we journey, through stories we mold,
On these soft pillows, our dreams manifold.

Repose in the Celestial Meadow

Beneath the stars, where whispers sigh,
The moonlight dances in the sky.
Soft petals rest on gentle breeze,
In harmony, the heart finds ease.

A tranquil place, where dreams are spun,
The night embraces everyone.
Each blade of grass, a secret told,
In silence, life's true beauty unfolds.

Crickets chirp a lullaby sweet,
While shadows play in moonlit suite.
With every breath, a peace descends,
In this meadow, time suspends.

Awake, yet lost in gentle sleep,
The soul rejoices, calm and deep.
To linger here is pure delight,
In the celestial soft twilight.

Floating in the Ether's Lullaby

On clouds of silk, we drift and sway,
In whispers soft, the night holds sway.
Stars like jewels in velvet night,
Guide our dreams, a soothing light.

Ethereal songs of heaven's grace,
Embrace our hearts in this vast space.
With every note, our worries cease,
In this realm, we find our peace.

A dance of shadows, dreams intertwined,
In this moment, our souls aligned.
Floating free, the world below,
In unity, our spirits glow.

The softness of the night enfolds,
As timeless stories softly unfold.
Through ether's charm, we gently glide,
In lullabies, our hearts abide.

Soaring with Midnight's Caress

In twilight's arms, we rise and roam,
With every heartbeat, we find home.
Midnight's kiss upon our skin,
Unveils the magic deep within.

Soaring high, where silence reigns,
Our spirits free from earthly chains.
With starlit paths, we carve the night,
In dreams anew, we take our flight.

A tapestry of dark and light,
Guides us through the velvet night.
With every breath, our worries fade,
In midnight's arms, our fears are laid.

The winds of change, they softly sing,
In this embrace, we find our wings.
Soaring high through endless skies,
In midnight's caress, our spirits rise.

Restful Adventures in Ethereal Heights

In realms above, where stardust flows,
Ethereal paths where no one knows.
Journeys paint the skies with light,
Adventure waits, a pure delight.

With every step, our dreams ignite,
Through sacred halls of cosmic night.
Floating softly, we embrace the call,
In restful heights, we conquer all.

The universe sings a gentle song,
Guiding us where we belong.
Whispers of promise fill the air,
In adventures vast, we find our care.

In tranquil spaces, our hearts will soar,
To explore what life has in store.
Restful journeys, hand in hand,
In ethereal heights, forever we stand.

The Cradle of Celestial Sleep

In a hush of twilight's glow,
Soft winds whisper, hearts in tow.
Stars emerge in velvet skies,
Cradling dreams where silence lies.

Moonlight dances on soft streams,
Lulling spirits into dreams.
Resting gently in the night,
Wrapped in peace, devoid of fright.

Clouds drift softly, shadows bend,
In this realm where sorrows end.
Here, the realms of sleep are vast,
Nestled in the night's embrace, steadfast.

Awake to morning's light anew,
With dreams as fresh as morning dew.
In the cradle, let hopes leap,
Find your solace, safe in sleep.

Soaring Into Silent Dreams

On wings of night, we gently glide,
Through expansive realms where dreams reside.
Stars above, like lanterns glow,
Guiding hearts where thoughts can flow.

The silence wraps us in its grace,
In ethereal skies, our thoughts embrace.
Each moment sways, a tender kiss,
Soaring high in the quiet bliss.

Whispers echo in the dark,
As we search for that fleeting spark.
Together we drift, hand in hand,
Across the canvas, dreams expand.

With every breath, the night we trace,
In the stillness, we find our place.
Soaring through the silent streams,
We awaken, painting future dreams.

Echoes of Feathered Thoughts

Amongst soft whispers of the trees,
Lies a world where thoughts find ease.
Feathers drift on gentle air,
Carrying wishes, light as a prayer.

Echoes of voices, sweet and light,
Flutter by in the fading night.
With every rustle, stories weave,
In the silence, hearts believe.

Thoughts take flight on wings of hope,
In the shadows, they learn to cope.
Every sigh becomes a song,
In this realm, we all belong.

As dawn breaks, the echoes fade,
Yet the memories never trade.
Feathered thoughts in morning's light,
Guide us gently, take us higher.

Cumulus Castles

Up above in skies so wide,
Cumulus castles softly glide.
Pillowy forms, where dreams take shape,
In this realm, we're free to escape.

With every cloud, a story spins,
Of laughter shared and quiet grins.
A kingdom built on gentle air,
Where worries vanish, light as prayer.

Through sunlight's kiss and shadows cast,
In these castles, joy will last.
Drifting high, with hearts so light,
We dance on clouds, with sheer delight.

As evening falls, the colors blend,
Our journey knows no bounds, no end.
In cumulus dreams, we find our way,
A world of hope at the close of day.

Raindrop Reveries

Gentle drops begin to fall,
A symphony on rooftops called.
Whispers soft, a lullaby,
Nature's tears will never dry.

Puddles form, a mirror's face,
Dancing light in liquid grace.
Each connection, fleeting spark,
In the silence, life’s remark.

Clouds like dreams float overhead,
Bearing stories yet unsaid.
With every splash, a memory,
Of calmness found in reverie.

The world renewed with every drop,
As time seems slow, then fast, then stop.
In raindrop dreams, we find our peace,
A fleeting moment, sweet release.

Floating Among Wispy Thoughts

A feathered breeze caresses skin,
With whispers soft, the day begins.
Thoughts like clouds drift high above,
Embracing peace, embracing love.

In the vastness, ideas bloom,
Spirits rise, dispelling gloom.
Each notion hangs like morning mist,
Chasing dreams we can't resist.

Close your eyes, let go of fear,
Listen to the silence near.
Floating high on currents light,
Finding solace in the flight.

Beneath the sky, we weave our song,
In wispy thoughts, we all belong.
Embracing all that makes us whole,
A dance of dreams that fills the soul.

Satin Dreams Adrift

Soft and smooth, the night unfolds,
In satin dreams, a story told.
Whispers weave through twilight skies,
As starlit visions gently rise.

Laces twine in silver light,
With every heartbeat, pure delight.
Floating softly on the seams,
We’re cradled in our woven dreams.

Midnight calls with velvet voice,
Promising the heart’s rejoice.
In tranquil space, we come alive,
As fantasies begin to thrive.

Awash in shades of soft embrace,
Each moment filled with quiet grace.
Satin dreams, forever swift,
A precious, fleeting, timeless gift.

Envelopes of Elysium

Sealed with care, the whispers flow,
Envelopes of dreams bestowed.
In hidden realms, the magic speaks,
As heart and soul, the silence seeks.

Golden light spills through the seams,
Cradling softly our wildest dreams.
With every crease, a new design,
Elysium calls, the stars align.

Contours of hope, paths intertwine,
Wrapped in solace, divine design.
Moments cherished, never lost,
In these letters, we count the cost.

Unfold the truths, let courage soar,
In envelopes of ancient lore.
Embrace the journey, let it unfold,
For in our hearts, the stories told.

Ethereal Slumbering Wonders

In twilight's hush, the dreams unfold,
Where whispers dance in silence bold.
Celestial beams of silver light,
Guide wanderers through the night.

In gentle realms, the shadows play,
Embracing secrets, soft as clay.
Stars weave tales with twinkling grace,
In slumber's arms, we find our place.

Floating on clouds of tender thought,
In realms where vivid dreams are caught.
A tapestry of night-time spells,
In whimsical waves, our spirit dwells.

Beyond the veil, reality bends,
In tranquil spheres, where magic descends.
Ethereal wonders call our name,
In soul's embrace, we'll never be the same.

Serenity in a Soft Infinity

Softly draped in twilight's glow,
Where time and space begin to flow.
A quiet hush, the world pauses,
In soft infinity, love causes.

Embracing moments, sweet and rare,
With every breath, we feel the air.
A gentle breeze through summer's trees,
Whispers secrets, brings us ease.

Nestled in warmth, hearts intertwine,
The universe feels so divine.
In silence, a melody begins,
A soft refrain of life's true wins.

Together we find our perfect peace,
Where worries fade, and sorrows cease.
In serenity's soft embrace,
We dance through life, with love and grace.

Daydreamer's Airborne Retreat

Floating high on clouds of thought,
In daydreams vast, our hearts are caught.
Wings unfurl in the azure sky,
Where fantasies and hopes can fly.

Drifting through fields of gentle sighs,
Where sunlit whispers never die.
In sweet escapades, we find a way,
To live forever in the play.

Chasing shadows, light as air,
Through vibrant dreams that we can share.
With every breath, we take to flight,
In daydream's realm, everything feels right.

A symphony of laughter rings,
In this retreat, our spirit sings.
With each horizon, new paths call,
In the daydreamer's world, we give our all.

Lulling into Luminous Stillness

In twilight's cradle, stillness reigns,
Luminous whispers fill the planes.
The gentle waves of evening start,
As peace encircles every heart.

With closed eyes, we drift away,
Into the dawn of another day.
Where light meets dark, the magic spins,
In lulling rhythms, the calm begins.

Stars awaken, twinkle bright,
Guiding souls through the velvet night.
A melody of dreams unspun,
Cradled softly till night is done.

In this moment of pure delight,
We find our way through the endless night.
Luminous stillness, forever ours,
In gentle ways beneath the stars.

Cushions of Infinity

Softest whispers cradle dreams,
Drifting in a gentle stream.
Stars above in velvet skies,
Hold our hopes as time flies.

Night descends with a tender sigh,
A place where silenced wishes lie.
Feathers of light drift and sway,
Guiding souls in a cosmic ballet.

Beneath the glow of moonlit beams,
We wander through our quiet themes.
Each cushion holds a secret bright,
Carrying us into the night.

In this realm where silence reigns,
Infinite echoes, unbroken chains.
We rest where time dares not to tread,
On cushions where the dreams are fed.

Slumbering Above the Ordinary

Clouds embrace the afternoon,
Painting skies with a soft tune.
As daylight fades, we soar high,
Slumbering where the eagles fly.

Mountains tower, guardians bold,
Whisper stories yet untold.
In this space, the heart finds peace,
From worldly noise, a sweet release.

Gentle winds, like secrets shared,
Wrap around the dreams prepared.
Above the fray, we find our place,
In tranquil heights of boundless grace.

Stars will guide the way tonight,
Flickering with a cosmic light.
In this slumber, we are free,
Above the ordinary, just we.

Chasing Wisps of Serenity

Dancing leaves in golden hues,
Carry whispers of morning dews.
In the stillness, hearts ignite,
Chasing dreams that take to flight.

Gentle streams weave stories old,
In their currents, secrets unfold.
With each babble, a symphony,
Inviting souls to wander free.

Sunset paints the sky in fire,
As day surrenders to desire.
With each twinkling, hope is born,
In the quiet of early morn.

Through the mist, we chase and spin,
Finding peace where journeys begin.
In the silence, we can see,
The wisps of our serenity.

The Tapestry of Daydreams

Threads of gold in twilight's weave,
Craft a world that we believe.
Every thought a stitch in time,
Woven softly, pure as rhyme.

Scattered colors, bright and bold,
Tales of love and dreams unfold.
In this fabric, hearts entwine,
Embracing visions, pure design.

Clouds like canvases above,
Brush the skies with strokes of love.
Every moment, vivid, true,
A tapestry that starts with you.

In daydreams where our spirits play,
We find ourselves in bright array.
Each story threads a piece of heart,
In this creation, we’re a part.

A Reverie Above the World

In whispers soft the breezes play,
They lift my thoughts and drift away.
With clouds as dreams and skies so bright,
I find my peace in gentle flight.

A canvas painted, hues unwind,
Elysian realms where stars align.
The world below, a distant sound,
In blissful thoughts, I'm safely bound.

Between the clouds, my heart will soar,
Through realms of magic, evermore.
I dance on winds, a spirit free,
My soul's delight, the sky's decree.

A reverie that knows no end,
In lofty heights where dreams transcend.
Above the world, I drift and glide,
In twilight's glow, my hopes reside.

Slumber’s Gentle Embrace

Nestled deep in twilight’s grace,
The shadows weave a soft embrace.
With lullabies that cradle dreams,
The world dissolves in whispered themes.

A gentle sigh, the night unfolds,
In velvet dark, the heart consoles.
Each fleeting thought, like stardust glints,
In slumber's arms, the spirit hints.

The moonlight bathes the weary soul,
In peaceful waves, it finds its role.
With every breath, the worries fade,
In soft cocoon, my thoughts cascade.

As dreams unravel, dark and light,
I drift through realms of pure delight.
In slumber’s hold, I find my place,
A tranquil heart in night's embrace.

Dreamscapes in the Sky

Above the clouds where visions play,
I wander softly, night and day.
With stars as guides, I seek to find,
The magic realms where peace unwind.

A tapestry of endless hues,
In dreamscapes bright, the heart renews.
Where rivers flow with silver light,
And whispers of the stars ignite.

Each fleeting thought is set to fly,
In realms where wishes never die.
I chase the echoes of the night,
In dreamscapes vast, my heart takes flight.

A journey wrapped in softest glow,
Through skies of wonder, I shall go.
These dreamscapes in the sky unfold,
A timeless tale forever told.

Serenity Wrapped in Cotton

Wrapped in layers, soft and warm,
A gentle shelter from the storm.
In cotton dreams where time stands still,
I find a peace, a tranquil thrill.

The world outside, a distant hum,
In cozy corners, dreams will come.
A silent place where worries cease,
In whispered tones, I find my peace.

Each thread a bond, each stitch a heart,
In warmth cocooned, we're never apart.
Here, moments linger, softly spun,
In cotton realms, we come undone.

Serenity flows like liquid gold,
In gentle folds, our dreams unfold.
Wrapped in cotton, lost in grace,
In every hug, I find my place.

Serenity in the Stratosphere

High above the world below,
Where whispers touch the stars,
Calm waves of azure light,
In stillness, peace imbues.

Gentle currents cradle dreams,
As silence envelops the night,
Each breath a soft embrace,
In this tranquil, endless flight.

Clouds like cotton castles rise,
Beneath the vast expanse,
In quietude, the heart beats slow,
Each moment a timeless dance.

Here in the stratosphere's hold,
Life's troubles drift away,
A sanctuary, a haven found,
In shimmering skies of gray.

Dreamweaving in the Clouds

Threads of thought, a gentle weave,
In the sky, they twist and twine,
Cotton clouds, a tapestry,
Reflecting dreams, pure and divine.

Colors blend in warm embrace,
Each hue a story to share,
Wandering whispers dance in light,
As fantasies float in the air.

Softly cradling the day's hopes,
Breathable as summer rain,
In the still, enchanted dusk,
Life's wonders softly remain.

Weaving dreams, the stars align,
With heartbeats, hopes combine,
In every drift across the sky,
A world of magic we define.

A Fleeting Stillness Above

A moment caught in time's embrace,
Where stillness hovers, light as air,
Above the chaos of the ground,
A gentle hush, a serene prayer.

Wings of silence softly glide,
Through endless azure, vast and wide,
Inviting peace, a fleeting grace,
In solitude, we find our place.

Here in the heights, our worries fade,
Bathed in the glow of twilight's hue,
The heart, unburdened, dares to soar,
In this realm where dreams come true.

Moments blend as shadows play,
Above where fleeting breezes sigh,
In quiet calm, life's treasures bloom,
A soothing balm against the high.

Embracing the Softness

In tender whispers, breezes roam,
Caressing skin with gentle grace,
Embracing softness all around,
Encircling hearts in a warm place.

The clouds, a quilt of silken dreams,
Swaddling illusions with delight,
In the hush of twilight's glow,
We find the stars align just right.

Each sigh a tender lullaby,
A promise wrapped in cotton threads,
Underneath the endless sky,
Softly weaving what dreams embed.

Here, we linger, hand in hand,
In a world where time stands still,
Embracing all that life can gift,
In every breath, we taste the thrill.

Escaping to Ether Realms

In twilight's gentle glow, we drift,
Beyond the world, our spirits lift.
With stars as guides, we wander free,
In ether realms, just you and me.

Light whispers call from distant light,
Through cosmic paths, we chase the night.
The moon's soft song, a lullaby,
In dreams we dance, as time slips by.

Winds of change sweep through our souls,
As magic stirs and softly tolls.
Transcending earth's weight, we embrace,
The boundless void, a vast, warm space.

Together lost, yet never found,
In ether's grasp, we spin around.
With every breath, we soar and dive,
In silent bliss, we are alive.

Breezy Respite of the Soul

Amidst the pines, I hear a tune,
Soft breezes hum, like summer's bloom.
The sun dips low, the day takes flight,
In nature's arms, I find pure light.

A gentle breeze, my spirit sways,
In dappled shade, I seek the days.
With each soft rustle, worries cease,
In this calm haven, I find peace.

Clouds float by, a dreamy sight,
Each fleeting thought feels warm and bright.
I close my eyes, embrace the air,
A breezy respite, beyond compare.

Moments linger, sweet and slow,
As whispers dance, they ebb and flow.
My heart expands, the world so whole,
In quiet grace, I soothe my soul.

The Garden of Soft Clouds

In a garden high, where clouds drift low,
Petals of white in the sunlight's glow.
Whispers of dreams on a soft, warm breeze,
Here, in this haven, the heart finds ease.

Golden rays touch each fluffy mound,
As laughter echoes, light and profound.
In twilight gardens, stars bloom bright,
Guiding the wanderers into the night.

Each gentle puff, a memory made,
In this soft space, worries do fade.
Hearts intertwine as we rise and roam,
In the garden of clouds, we find our home.

With fleecy patches beneath our feet,
The world is hushed; our souls are sweet.
Here, sun and moon take turns to play,
In the garden of clouds, we forever stay.

Voyage of the Sleepy Spirits

In twilight's hush, the spirits glide,
On silver sails, where dreams abide.
With whispers soft, they float and sway,
In the ocean of night, they drift away.

Stars their compass in skies of deep,
Through realms unknown, the weary sleep.
A voyage grand, on waves of light,
They dance with shadows, taking flight.

Soulful echoes of stories told,
In every drift, a heart of gold.
They chase the dawn with tender grace,
In the arms of slumber, they find their place.

As night unwinds and curtains fall,
The sleepy spirits hear the call.
On mystic winds, they soar and spin,
In the voyage of dreams, all journeys begin.

Drowsy Dreams Above the Horizon

Soft whispers call my name,
Drifting gently, free from pain.
Clouds embrace the fading light,
In this realm, all feels so right.

Golden hues of dawn break free,
Painting skies with blissful glee.
Close my eyes, I start to sway,
Finding peace till break of day.

Snoozing Amidst the Stars' Glow

Wrapped in twilight's warm embrace,
Floating softly through pure space.
Stars above begin to dance,
Inviting me to take a chance.

Galaxies whisper secrets sweet,
As dreams and stardust intertwine.
In this cosmic, soothing beat,
I find solace, pure, divine.

Laid Back in Luxe Stratosphere

High above the world I stand,
Where soft clouds cradle every hand.
Lounge upon this gentle air,
Weightless, free without a care.

Golden rays of sun pour down,
In this quiet, I won't drown.
Peace surrounds like softest silk,
Time stands still, a dreamlike milk.

Serene Escape on Airy Pillows

Pillows made of cotton dreams,
Where tranquility softly beams.
Resting here, I gently sway,
Letting worries drift away.

The world below fades from view,
Lost in thoughts of skies so blue.
Serenity wraps ‘round my soul,
In this space, I've found my whole.

Milton Keynes UK
Ingram Content Group UK Ltd.
UKHW020903041224
451843UK00022B/127

9 789916 906903